Watching the Worlds Go By

Selected Poems
By

Omar S. Pound

Panther Creek Press
Spring, Texas

Published by Panther Creek Press
SAN 253-8520
116 Tree Crest Circle
P.O. Box 130233, Panther Creek Station
Spring, Texas 77393-0233
Cover print and interior illustrations © William H. Laufer
Cover design by Pamela Copus, Sonic Media
Plano, Texas

Manufactured in the United States of America
Printed and bound by Data Duplicators, Inc.
Houston, Texas

1 2 3 4 5 6 7 8 9 10

Library of Congress Cataloguing in Publication Data

Pound, Omar S.

        I. Title   II Poetry

ISBN 0-9678343-5-X

for Elizabeth

Lo! Man was created anxious.
Qur'an, LXX, verse 19.

إِنَّ الْإِنْسَانَ خُلِقَ هَلُوعًا

Table of Contents

Table of Contents, *continued*

Translations are noted by asterisks

The author gratefully acknowledges the following publishers and publications where some of these poems have appeared previously:

The Antigonish Review; Delta *(Montreal);* Exeter Books *(Exeter, England);* Fulcrum Press *(London);* Grosseteste Review *(Lincoln, England);* New Directions Publications *(New York);* Origin *(Kyoto, Japan);* Samphire *(Ipswich, England);* Writers Forum *(University of Colorado);* Migrant Press *(England);* Woolmer/Brotherson, Ltd., publishers of *Saint Erkenwald* and *Siege; Lucknow 1857 (Revere, PA);* Tarlane Editions, publishers of *The Dying Sorcerer (Antigonish, Nova Scotia);* National Poetry Foundation, University of Maine, and Three Continents Press (Washington, D.C.); the Strawberry Press (London); Alharaka Alshiriya Books;The LaNana Creek Press (Nacogdoches, TX)

Introduction

The aim of this collection is to make a generous cross-section of Omar Pound's poetry available to a wide audience. The veteran Pound reader will recognize some favorites but will also find new poems scattered among them. Two, "Tsunami" and "Mama," were completed during the proofing stages of this book.

The selections are mine, with the assistance of William Laufer, whose art appears inside, as well as on the cover. Poem placement was at my whim, their order having no significance as to my favorites. Were that the case, then "Saint Erkenwald" might very well begin or end the collection. I came upon the poem late in the selection process and pounced upon it as a touchstone of many of the characteristics I enjoy most. Pound is frequently a story-teller, and one is likely to learn a thing or two as the narrative unfolds. Foremost is his carefully muted scholarship, concealed as a rule by a layer of humor. In this case, he has taken a two-paragraph reference from Bede's *Ecclestical History of the English People* about a 7th century bishop of the East Saxons named Earconwald and has spun out a likely--or unlikely--narrative of his activities before and after his death. If one detects a wry note of skepticism, then so much the better.

Although many selections betray the poet's social conscience, Pound often approaches his subject in a tentative sidle, doubt doctored with puckish wit. An empathetic bent allows him to don personae of any ilk, from a variety of regions and eras, but his attention to detail makes the performance believable. Thus, in "Siege, Lucknow 1857," while recounting the day's injuries and deaths, the narrator keeps tabs on the price of Brandy in the embattled camp and notes his son's eighth birthday back in Dundee: "Eight so soon,/...and dining downstairs on Sundays."

For sheer fun there is "Pissle and the Holy Grail" starring

Sir Parzifal's horse, Pissle, whose birth, along with that of the narrator William, is the subject of the poem's first section, appearing in this volume.

Pound's lyrics must include some of his many translations from the Arabic and Persian, not only for their own lyric voice, but because of their obvious influence on his other work.

As he watches the worlds go by, he ties the whole human experience into one ball of string, observing unflinching parallels across time, such as "The Peterloo Massacre Witnessed: Manchester (1819) or Kent State." Pound's shorter lyrics are sprinkled throughout, offering, I trust, pleasant surprises at every turn of the page, as yet another aspect of this insightful, impish, humble poet reveals itself.

Guida Jackson
The Woodlands, Texas
2001

.

Watching the Worlds Go By

Mama

Kennst du das Land
wo die Zitronen blühn?

Goethe

Where are all the lemon-trees gone
you still count me to sleep with?
where are the oranges and olives
for harvest-time?

We've only open sewers now
where nothing can be sown,
and tanks block muddy paths
to where Granny's cousins live,
and young men shoot at us
in training, it's only a game for them,
as we race round each corner
from hovel to hovel
for our ration of olive-oil
and a kilo of bread for eleven.

Why can't we go home
to sunny Palestine
with a cargo of grapes and olives
overflowing on heaped-up trays
to comfort cousin Hamid?
What is a permit? and why,
why can't we stay beside him
to help him die?

Was hat man dir, du armes Kind, getan?
What have they done to you, poor child
and why do none weep for you here?
They say they came to make the desert bloom,
then cut our olive trees down
and rooted up our orange groves.

None weep for you, my raisin-eyed one,
for power and greed are more dear to them
      than you can ever be.

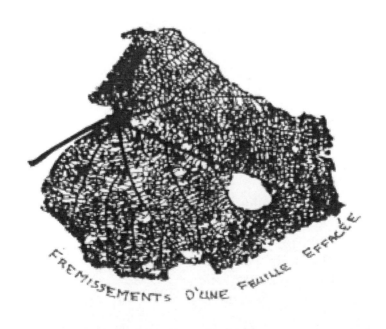

FREMISSEMENTS D'UNE FEUILLE EFFACÉE

The Monk's Revenge

Twenty-seven years or is it twenty-eight
worshipping -- with all that supererogation
I'm off, a throw-back into a life of sorts.

What is it prisoners do escaping the public nest
before the nightly count? Puff pillows into forms
beneath a blanket to fool the screws.
I've done that too, fooling none but me.

    I've a scarf to seem my head,
    a paper plate for halo,
    but who ever heard of a monk
    with a halo on in bed;
    for throat and neck, I'll invent. . .
    and at the heart's hollow
    there's nothing to hide.

As for the rest, I must choose belly down,
or facing up, uplifted -- but that posture
raises contours pillows can't concoct.
Then feet -- a crusader's,
    crossed and transfixed in stone,
    jabbing the future with his past.

For verisimilitude I'll leave *John 14* open:
I go now unto my Father . . .
Go to my father! That lowercase F!
That's why I came here first!
I was thin, too fragile for the world,
a monarch untonsured with a flaming head.

Before I go I must be willful once --
incense them with something malodorous;
a diced onion or shallot in the chalice,
the odor will soon absorb
their sanctimonious blessings
for one they think lost.
Lost indeed!
All their wanting of Heaven is greed enough
to send a man to Hell -- but to me, Dear Lord,
      their avarice is not enough.

Holyland

Notes: These poems were written while I was recovering from major cancer surgery. A FUTURE HISTORY OF THE GAZA STRIP and CAUSES OF HATE portray how grandmothers and great-grandmothers will tell future generations about the occupation; THE CORONER suggests what might have happened in the 20th century on finding a burial cave empty; THE PRODIGAL SON RETURNS TO THE 46TH FLOOR, NEW YORK tells of a New Yorker believing he went off to fight for his Faith as a paratrooper, returns to Wall Street where he also finds an empty world awaiting him, and commits suicide; TURPS tells of life in a refugee camp where everyone is trying to make a dishonest penny or two somehow.

Omar S. Pound
March 29, 2000

A Future History of the Gaza Strip

Actions children will always remember
are dangerous:
    troops overturning flower-pots,
    stealing salt,
    twisting my uncle's lameness into rubble;
    breaking in and pouring pepper
        into the coffee-bin;
    snatching sweetmeats from my youngest sister
    with sixty years more to come
    resenting that grab;
    bull-dozing fourteen homes
    shooting my mother's brother's nephew
    for stoning tanks with a sling-shot,
    eviscerating my little cousin
    for aiming a toy pistol
    at a convoy of jeeps,
        and
        shooting the cat.

Causes of Hate

On her 87th birthday auntie died,
(non-lethal tear-gas).
She always reminded us:
"The Turks were sometimes cruel
but never like this.
We'd serve them coffee
        they'd talk,
take some fruit and go."

Layla's baby almost choked too
but a water-soaked quilt
saved him. In ten years
he'll be stoning *them*
        until we're free.

The Coroner

After every death
there's paperwork to do.
"When did it happen?"
"Last Friday."
"Where's the body?"
"Hidden."
"Why?"
"We wanted it out of sight
      before the weekend
      safe from wolves
      grave-robbers and such."

That was a no-no!
"We simply wanted space for a wake
      to celebrate our joy."
That *was* suspicious,
'Possible foul play,'
      I noted down with pleasure.
"Again -- where did you put him?"
"Outside town."
"Go bring him in."
So we took him to a hillside cave
one we knew we had to use.

A small landslide after heavy rains
blocked the entrance.
'Nice peaceful spot, this,' I thought.
'Improperly buried,' I noted.
But they knew it was ordained
as is so much in life and beyond.

"Clear the rubble away
before another mishap hides the evidence.
I must, I repeat, must see the body,
and report any suspicious wounds,
internal bleeding, hemorrhage,
or broken bones."

They worked until the sun
        gave us its glow.
The cave was empty.
I'm not paid for overtime
so I went home, dissatisfied,
my suspicions almost verified.
But what could I do,
        on a Sunday at that.

The case never came to trial,
it's still on the books,
and has remained
      a Mystery
          ever since.

The Prodigal Son Returns
to the 46th Floor, New York

A volunteer paratrooper,
he compelled himself to merge
        his faith and politics
and stave off boredom:
        bankruptcies
        accounting
        and endless office antics.

Returning to nuances in estate taxes
from guarding seven bull-dozers
and three new settlements
Amos, aged forty-six,
with the blustering voice
of the readily depressed,
shouted from the window ledge
        "Leave me alone..."
a reminder of his solitude
in the air and sniping down below,
"I want the world to know
I died a nonentity;
my only honor: refusing honors
for shooting boys
they claimed were stoning
our captain's tank.

Turps

Last week we dragged the Thinner up,
heels first -- he refused to walk.
He'd been thinning out the olive oil
with I don't know what,
and poisoned Ahmad's family
three girls
    and both our grannies.
        Whatever it was
        turned their skin olive...
        and they all went bald...
        My mother's sister
        had said the oil 'smelt bad'.

The Thinner went before
    the moonlight lit the hilltop
        we had chosen.

Nelly and Ellen:
A Tale of Two Sisters

I

"It's your own darn fault marrying
that no-good composer-fellow.
Never made a penny,
brought you no pension,
even that flashy medal,
his second award,
was cast in bronze not gold,
glitter and no cash
and all that postage thanking
his scruffy friends
for their congrats.
Just as well he's gone
no more sponging off
that arty lot.

"I remember you all excited
when two Hungarian pianists
played something he wrote:
'great percussive vitality...'
one reviewer said,
whatever that means.
Just noisy, I'll guess.
They played for prestige
hating Terry's music,
or so Mrs. Small said.

"You should have done what I did,
marry a steady one,
twenty-three years older maybe,
but a real good provider

and look where I am,
now he's gone,
good pension, a place to live,
my cats love it, milk bill paid,
electricity due next week,
with more than enough to cover it.
My only bother: tax time,
forms I don't understand,
all those little boxes to mark
remind me of cheating at school.

"But my John was always doing
something useful
selling things people need
and good value at that,
shoes all the best leather
well-sewn, no complaints,
reasonable mark-up,
only 35% on weekdays
when husbands weren't home,
with adjustments at weekends
if he was in.

"I hear you're in a Home
you can't afford,
after Terry's friends
gathered around his favorite
drinking den whirling
a top hat on a conductor's baton
for contribs.
'Rally for Terry's Nelly' indeed!
You should be ashamed.
What'll I say to Mrs. Small
and the neighbors:
'Nelly's living on charity now.'

"And those two trumpeters,
foreigners at that, sitting
on the piano playing
for your birthday.
All that noise!
The nurses must have hated it.
Oh no! I hear the Home is so depraved
the patients loved it
and even the nurses
want them back."

II

Nelly died at 83, peacefully (they say)
but I'm not so sure about the aftermath.
Her two trumpeters played Vivaldi
and the Blues
for two hundred at the funeral,
leading a riotous march through town
to their favorite drinking-hole
'The Bubbling Vat.'
Who wants a funeral like that.

III

Ellen demanding more than any Home could provide
stayed in bed:
refusing to lift an arthritic leg.
The therapist, thwarted, had muttered:
"Ellen, you'll be bedridden,
you won't like that."
"But friends will visit me,
and take me out...."

For a while they did

21

consoling her with garden sprigs
in dusty jars from basements,
(nothing bought), but budding enough
to delay further visitations.

IV

Last Tuesday I wheeled her to the ward's
best bay window
to watch a jovial labrador
sniffing and circling
the base of a flowering cherry tree,
then suddenly, he dropped
his hurriedly remobilised leg
as a passing squirrel
changed pace and direction,
spiraling up a nearby tree
to twitch and watch
nature's futile ceremony:
dog, neck upward, all excited
scratching and whining in dismay.

Before the call to supper
he tours his ward,
wagging for cookies
lifting up a bedside paw
in humility and serenity
with occasional licks
for mobile friends
among the dying and the sick,
looking ever forward
to future visitations
ignoring those declining
his infectious
give-and-take.

Hong Kong: The Final Release

Dodging rickshaws and stubborn donkeys
heavy-breasted with loaded straw,
Sikh guards, turban-tall,
girls paired like pigtails,
I visit the bazaar to replace
the merchants' chanted chatterings
with whistles, croaks,
shrieks and yowls.

Birds from new Zealand,
Papua, New Guinea,
some sold in plastic bags,
    some in bamboo cages,
displaying feathered pigtails
in flashing beauty
        to no mates.

The Pu-ke-ko's monotone
of growling shrieking
cannot outwit the Ta-ka-he duets.
Even parrots hesitate, then preen
their beaks on bamboo bars,
before announcing
      in raucous shrieks
the coloring they sell, and finches,
passionately alert for market flies,
diet on delicacies no man desires
      or can destroy.

Near penniless I buy two singers
and a clowning parakeet ---
    walk to the hills,
      let them go, aware
their mercantile captivity
was too domestic
      for hawks to miss.

Omar S. Pound

Bangladesh: The Fates of Man

And of us all, one drowned in a ditch,
another a buffalo pierced, now only eats
when those who can work have fed.
Our eldest leads many,
      but in fearing feels his way,
        while the youngest holds his hand.
One flew from a cocoanut tree
      without feathers
        or a tail.

Muhammed donned a uniform
      to bring a pension home.
Hasan, angered by ale,
    goes to the gallows tomorrow
unless our bribe belittles my brother's.
Abdullah prospers in pleasure,
    his forbears forgotten.
Hamid, our last, may Allah be praised,
    craves power in parliament,
    and is powerless to care or cure.
But the One we love the most
        knows no grave.

Affection/Disaffection

Smokey's death has loosed my vocal chords.
I talk and talk and talk,
today I watered my winter plants twice
and fed his brother Snowy
at all his wrong times.

Thirty-four years ago, I shouted at my mother
"I won't have an animal in the house...."
"Oh yes, my dear, you will,
            just wait and see,"
she mumbled back with feline calm
            and determination.

When she died I moved
most of the furniture around
            trying to be useful,
an aftermath of the inevitable,
                        and
more soothing than any eulogistic Mass.

What Smokey would do without me
was always my fear, but life's
            a litter of catastrophes
            and I,
thickened humorless on the wheel
            of things I can't defeat,
and weeping because my eyes
            can only water now.

I think backwards
        to thirty-one years ago,
unraveling all his archings,
        wheedlings, and finally
            at snacktime
        protestations
        that he was never loved enough.
        But he knew my private world
        of widowhood and emptiness.

If my end will be where
I can still think of you
I'm ready to go.
Mother can take care of herself.

Kano

Grass-hut after grass-hut, Kano was founded.
Thanks be to Allah and the Prophet, whose heart,
split, its anger cut out,
                    emptied
        of all but deeds of light.

Tell of the mahogany tree where hunters first cooked and camped.
sharing lion and elephant. Vapours rose, men soon came,
a few with women trailing. Came new plaiting for the huts,
some tried mud but were laughed away. With women around
the dust-heap of disputes arose, hunting palled,
millet and sorghum acquired their seasons,
and only famine brought hunting back.

Came one who saw Kano had no wall,
another added fourteen towers, only the tallest crumbled in a
                                                flood,
but the Prowler came prowling. The builder of towers passed on.
Came another who castrated his brother, and Omar of Islam,
who furnaced the fire that defies extinction.
Generous with alms he gave forty years leadership and banned
                                        palm-wine.

Death came to some who were complacent and unprepared,
Daguchi reigned five months and grew very rich,
another proved brittle alone.
Under Kunkuna the world was uncertain,
Shekarau toyed with life. He forgot,
            and thought there was no passing on.

Came Sharifa who ruled from the saddle, spear at hand,
unable to relax he extended walls, set feathers to our arrows,
built drinking troughs for the blind.
Zaki made kingship remote, massed horses with gold quilting

27

while guards with ostrich plumes rebuked the people
and confidants arranged the diary of his day.

Daudi reigned nine years, then went to the Compound
where no talking and no excuses were allowed.
Then Suleiman, his pick-axe physic for hard ground,
threw out heresy, brought back pure Islam, and none dared loiter
in the town. In victory no orphan's heritage was taken,
no virgin prisoner held. Came Abdullah, slave of God,
death came and left nought of him but the telling. He was old.

This world is old, and old men let heavy weights fall.
He who'd make the world his favourite wife is a fool
in a frenzy to die. Instead, learn how kings, their tale near lost,
cleared scrub and bush and sat about the mahogany tree.

I heard all this from one who was said to know,
so pass it on without additions. Much talking
mars good works and lessens the reward. Besides,
the character of men is often in dispute.

Thus was Kano built, grass-hut beyond grass-hut
with thirteen ramparts on the outer wall.

****

[* Kano was a historic Hausa kingdom founded ca. A.D. 999 and
located in present-day northern Nigeria.]

From the Caucasus

Adapted from the Latin of Lucan (39-65 A.D.):
Prometheus on Caucasus

Let's hang Ruslan Chechniya
from jutting rock, outcrop or crag,
barbed wire holding him
to any ledge, for all to see,
but not too low for relatives
to cut him down
and then to celebrate his martyrdom
with wasted rifle shots,
echoing reminders of his loyalty
to the freedom of their cause.

"If we crumple him up
for none to see,
villagers will never
learn from that.

"We'll do what we always do,
around the neck - erect,
barbs will hold his weight
and breezes forge more fear.

"Eagles will surely get him,
even egrets may experiment
swooping into maturity,
his wrigglings
interesting enough
to strengthen their wings,
and stimulate their future flights
for nourishment.

"Entrails first
then softer parts,
as lions gouge a stomach out
and disembowel their kill."

Siege
Lucknow 1857

May 3rd
>The Seventh Native Cavalry mutinied today
>spearing, looting, burning,
>then cantering off to Delhi
>for more of same;
>firing our stables to draw us out,
>but the Brigadier'd have none of it!

Tuesday
>Sir Henry Havelock is here
>writing and sleeping in Mr. Gubbins' drawing-room,
>the new H.Q. for his Command.

Wednesday
>Mr. Lucas reported bitten or killed by his horse.
>Came back at dawn,
>an arm hanging loose.
>Mutineers or horse?
>Too busy to ask
>and not much use.

>Sergeant-Major and the Riding-Master
>quarrelled today about the use of a whip.
>One shot the other dead. Not sure which.

>"The English are very fond of fighting,"
>Corporal Kelly quipped,
>"especially when they're Irish."

>Major Gall's body found,
>he left in disguise for news
>from behind enemy lines,
>and perhaps to clear his name.
>Did a woman trap him again?

Mrs. Bird has smallpox and her twins are sickly.

July 23rd

Cawnpore relieved, we hear,
but sad, sad news:
Sir Henry Lawrence asked to be buried with his men
and died.

Saturday

Sepoys of the 4th and their
imported ladies unruly last night.

Fine sermon today at Brigade H.Q.
(Matthew 22)
on The Wedding Garment;
appropriate now.
Salvation is precarious at the best of times.

Another chimney down at dawn;
we are surrounded now, and the siege is on.

Thursday

More shrapnel in the drawing-room
and Miss Palmer's leg carried off.

Up all night
with water, tea, and brandy
for gentlemen at the bailey
ordered to sleep at their posts,
or when they can.

Friday

Again the drawing-room hit
and dear Sir Henry's leg
ripped open near the hip.

Miss Palmer died,
but was buried with her other leg intact.
Thank God for small mercies;
The Lord will provide.

Grape-shot roughed up Capt. Fraser's hat this noon,
but later, he and Duncan sortied,
firing several houses the snipers used.

A busy day
two shots at breakfast-time,
three plates broken in their rack,
a distracting way to start the day.

William overworked, his hair falling out.
Must doctors always live with the dying
and the itchy?

No news of the Relief. Will it ever come?
Hope deferred makes the heart so ill.

Three more bairns buried at dusk,
One Catholic and two Chapel.

Sir Henry Lawrence supplies auctioned today:
Beer: 70 rupees a doz.,
Brandy: 160 for ten,
macaroni 55 rupees a packet,
and champagne only 50.

Sunday
The Lucas house blown up at sermon-time,
Capt. Fulton swears sweetly
his timing kept
Sunday snipers away!

Tuesday
Brandy 17 rupees a bottle,
and tobacco one rupee a leaf.

Thursday
The glint on Capt. Fulton's telescope
got him at dusk.

He'll hate his funeral--'too much fuss.'

William shot bringing an injured sepoy in.
Dear God. Don't take him from us.
What would we do without his doctoring.

Lucas came by to see him,
declining to drink
from my meagre store
of camomile tea.

Another sale today

Property belonging to sundry deceased.
Brandy up to 20.

Thursday

Further sale:
With more dead, prices are lower
and even soap is down.

Sept. 25th

Much firing tonight,
women and children screaming,
smoke, looting, and wild musketry,
but nothing near us.
two elephants heard trumpeting,
scared by the rushing and banging,
and sporadic shooting from afar,

and the distant sound
of drum and fife;
the bagpipes' drone;
the fife and drum,
Relief has come.
Thank God. The Relief has come.
May we all see Dundee again,
dear God, if you please.

Yesterday's looting brought the servants back,
with cloth and stuffs cheap.

Willie's brother is here with the Relief.
Came in weary,
a bullock had trampled him
and the tea he'd brought,
outside what used to be the dairy.

Must write to mother and my darlings in Dundee,
Donald's eight tomorrow,
and dining downstairs on Sundays, I suppose.
He'd be proud of his father doctoring on,
despite his wound and limp left arm.

Heroism and folly . . .
Now we are free to doubt again . . .

Eight so soon,
. . . and dining downstairs on Sundays.

NUNC FORTUNAS SUM*

* *"We are in luck now!"*

A Stone-Cutter to His Daughter

I know you may be dying
so beware of those who prophesy
your Resurrection. I'm too old,
    and you too young, for all that.

And in return I promise you
    no seances
        seeking you as aftermath.
Of course bits of you may last,
        many years perhaps,
beneath the stone I plan to carve, and,
        just in case I drop too soon,
            chisel in hand,
I'll cut first a cross, even before
        your name's incised,
not for Christ
        but all the joy I've lost.

Omar S. Pound

One Final Fling

Wind in your hair
my palms and fingers plough
through and through and through.
Oh God! Live for ever
      young and beautiful.

My fingers plough . . .

You turn my winter into spring
and all I bring: tears for lips
that hold my tongue. Stay young
even if not for me, stay young.

Soon you must go
and leave me living
like the blind
feeling but the edge of things
until my final burst
of dying brings
the luxury of death,
      before I grow unkind.

                Kemal Khojand (Persian)
                died 1401

Lament for a Magician

It's good to die before you want to,
but why did you have to go?
My mind, drifting like bait . . .
a leopard went hunting,
    its lozenges like stars
its eyes were golden snow.

But why did you have to die
with thirty thousand leopards in the sky?

It's so unfair,
    when I had planned a walk with you,
to watch you sport your country senses,
and hear you seeing Nature courting thought,
    where Nature knows no doubt . . .
and by the river sit
    reflecting our reflections
    the way the willow swings,
    fragile as resilient glass
        draining our watered paradise.

That was more than was good for us,
    with me waiting,
always in the underside of night,
waiting for the night those lozenges
    of golden snow would melt
        or leave you moribund,
the night the Gods
    reclaimed their loan of you,
and drained from me their Paradise.

Some of the women sat sewing
while others sharpened stones
the day St. Stephen died.

The First Supper

And as we ate
    Peter pushed his platter nearer,
not to hear better,
        but to let the warmth of shyness
            glow.

Samson

My eyes have lost their hold on day
and cannot find the night;
they harbor waves,
    and turn with the tides.
whatever storms they bring,
and even find the night at dawn;
while I await
    the unreflecting beams
you bring ashore
    into my blinding night.

Crimson maple leaves
on snow.
First blood to winter!

The Moral Majority: 848-9 A.D.

And nowadays
all honor orthodoxy
(never doubted before, of course!)
the right to overpower,
throw innovators from all heights,
and those disgraced by God
are fired like bricks
some red, some brown,
to crumble as they must;
apostate heads soon severed,
while gardens thrive on breath
apostles and believers give,
and pools reflect, through us,
       all Paradise.

      from Al-Suyuti (Arabic)

Traders in Beauty and Delight

You want a soothing life
all beauty and no worry,
what's sweeter then
than writing poetry?

Misfortune rakes poets
they gulp ill-luck
cup after cup
till broke
then turn to slavery
to stave off bankruptcy
and buy a winter coat.

Try buying slaves instead
trading in rounded breasts
or manly gestures,
a profit's sure
no need to borrow
nothing to store or kill
a wedding every night,
the merchandise for sale
                tomorrow.

                from Abu Dulama (Arabic)
                died 776/7?

for agnes bedford

Granada (ca. 1000 A.D.)

One after another
my contemporaries die,
I know I shall not live forever
but even as I touch
the coffin's cotton quilt
I feel so far from them
I cannot even choose
to be a looker-on,
but only see as one
who suddenly awakes
and walks with eyes
still shut, towards the light.

Another funeral done
now back to my hut
with wolves nearby
far safer than friends at court
where my contemporaries
all seem to die.

I remember leaving them
times were so unjust
those first were never men of worth
and those last, for ever
pushing on and up, were worse.
So I stayed aloof
finding none I'd care
to share my supper with
        or an evening prayer.

And now some younger ones
from the city come bustling in
saying it isn't right
that I, a learned man,
should end thu;.

So they fuss
about a house for me,
well-meaning I suppose
and it's nice to have some,
especially the young,
respectful at last, even though
they sometimes interrupt a doze.

But they don't understand,
my hut's more than enough
for one soon to die.

Tomorrow I'll tell them again:
but for summer heat, and rain,
occasional thieves in my garden,
and odds and ends the women need,
I'd build myself a spider's house;
I won't mention that my hands
are too arthritic to weave.

                    Abu Ishaq Al-Ilbiri
                    died 1067

The Rake

an imitation of abu nuwas (747?-815?)

Abandoned camps
pineapple breasts untouched
camels too young to die in battle
boys grown hairy
stallions lost
lovers parting with caravans at dawn;
Nuts! That's all stuff for poetry,
            unlike my sorrow.

For be there any sorrow more than mine?
The Prophet, may his name be ever blessed,
bans wine, and worse
            the magistrates enforce it.

Mix it with tears
yours
mine
I don't care whose
I'll drink and wait
nightwatchmen to pick me up
and bastinado me;
      guardians of my purity.

Fools, why not let me be,
drinking with every toy in town,
            don't thwart Allah
the world would end tomorrow
with you regretting purity,
while I will surely be
worthy of His Clemency.

                              Arabic

To a Hunchback

It is no fault to be deformed
drawn ligaments create the crescent moon
the viol's curvature rewards
nights and feasts with song and sleep
the bow's more feared than Christian sword
and scimitar more sure,
the camel with a swollen hump studs most
and only prows can split the waves.

The gods endow you hunchbacks
        with virtues
as hillocks on a mountain-top
and women, when they see
such superfluities,
devote themselves to men
      who
        arch
          like
      you.

Ibn al-Rumi (Arabic)
(836-896)

From
The Birth of Pissle and William the Narrator

Part One of Pissle and The Holy Grail

The night I was born another's barn was filled
    with lanterns, villagers and new-mown hay,
incantations and spring waters
    cleansed of all sprites.
Leather aprons and woollen skirts were laid about
to warm the earth and welcome our hero's birth.

By dawn, Winnie, his mother, had teased him forth,
and by noon all priestly offices performed,
had named him Puzzat and his pedigree declared,
and being winter, with nothing much to do,
all waited to watch him stand,
    wobbly at first, unsure,
    shake his head at our applause,
then slowly sink
    to learn the loyalty of milk to young.
What wealth was weaned. What joy!

Meanwhile Greta, my mother, lay on boards
in her truckle-bed, attended by two blind crones,
because the village knew I'd be a girl,
    deformed, if born at all,
because three black cats had spayed a hare at dawn
    the day my father left to win
    a Papal blessing in Jerusalem.
But someone had blundered. That hare
    had several generations in her loin,
so I was a boy 'William'. . . a common name,
'so he can live in peace unnoticed and unknown',

and, but for this tale, I was never known again.
    Sometimes the Gods are kind to men.

All the girls loved Puzzat as Pissle,
as much for his name as for himself,
so we let it be, and watched them greeting him
    with open arms and legs.
Stroking and brushing his heaving sides,
    they bartered silks for turns
to grip his flanks between their thighs
    and ride across the field, contented.

The older women watered and bedded him down in
                                                straw,
with woollen skirts and blankets warming
    the ground beneath them all.

Meanwhile I still hid inside their layers
of petticoats, 'til told to warm myself elsewhere,
so I danced with bulrushes and almost drowned,
    and let imagination stretch and dare
    where doings could not reach.
    But they collared me for chores,
    hunting herbs and bees,
    picking astringent celadine,
    harnessed to harvests,
    brewing beer and melting grease,
    wood for winter, sorting seeds.
I needed no dog, all barked at me.

I suffered the perils of joy and pleasure,
    nightmares and dreams,
    learned to mix egg-white with mill-dust,
    set fractured bones,

use goose-quills for many a broken nose,
saw polyps off with knotted thread, and more.

I watched Celtic carpenters construct carts
    for only the dead and rich,
    saw hawks stun rabbits with a talon tap,
and colored horse-hair lines for fish.

And soon I knew codpiece from crupper,
    breastplate from girth,
    bridal wreath from halter.
That caused laughter
      and not a little grief.

A few years later we heard my father's fate:
a rampart
    a ladder
      a Blessed Fall,
        worthy of Adam,
long before loot from Byzantium
      or glory at Jerusalem.
After that Greta never spoke again
    and soon grew fat.

Father had left us little, but Pissle stayed,
a name the future framed,
but only because Parsifal found him straying
where trees are sometimes Gods
      and sometimes men;
loved him on sight, kissed his forelock,
threw his arms around his neck,
      mounted him and fled.

Through ruts cut clean by carts
they trekked, Pissle and Parsifal,
looking for what my little cousin Maria
    called a stirrup-cup.

Time, like an adder, slithered by,
I watched many save and many steal,
saw men banished to sundew bogs,
learned not to anger women,
    or laugh at jealousy,
and saw why breath and men soon part.

One day I too found it wise to leave,
so I joined Parsifal and Pissle rather hastily,
    which is how I come to tell this tale.

Carmina Burana

The following synopsis of the choral drama by Carl Orff (b. 1895) was prepared by Omar Pound for a Cambridge Philharmonic Society concert held November 28, 1978 (U.K.).

Carmina Burana was first performed in 1937. The title literally means "Songs of Benediktbenern", a monastery in the Bavarian Alps where a Latin codex of thirteenth-century songs was discovered. The collection is songs and poems by,among others, jesters and minstrels,touching on every aspect of human experience. "Fortuna Imperatrix Mundi" means "Fortune Empress of the World."

Fortuna Imperatrix Mundi
1. *O Fortuna*
O Fortune, O Fortune
like a moon, full and new
now kind, now wistful
a dangling jewel.

Whether pockets are empty
or a crown on the head,
you melt both like ice
turning joy to dread.

Weep for me, friends
she's cunning and cruel
weep for me, all,
and despair at her rule,
Fortune, O Fortune
I despair of your rule.

2. *Fortune plango vulnera*

Once a king to every girl
now a thug to all the world,
no hair where once was heavy thatch,
caught by Time, when I, even I,
was once the catch.

I. Primo Vere
3. *Veris leta facies*
Spring has won again
and winter's army gone,
plovers, girls and trees awake
alert for love and song.
Hear them singing, chant and giggle,
weaving welcomes for the Spring.
Gaudeamus, let us sing!
Spring, the sweet Spring.
4. *Omnia Sol temperat*
5. *Ecce gratum*
The sun is true, as I to you
bring joy beyond all winter's sadness.
Pity the man for whom the sun
invokes no lechery and lewdness.

Uf dem Anger
6. *Tanz*
7. *Floret silva nobilis*
8. *Chramer, gip die varwe mir*
The forest fills with flowers
and leaves are yellow-green
but last year's love has not come back,
even his horse has not been seen.
Who will love me now
when everywhere is Spring?

The forest's new, so I will, too,
with rouge and other fancies
grace myself to please anew
and practice all my glances.
Come, young men, come!
Now even I am Spring again.
9. *Reie*
Swaz hie gat umbe
Chume, chum geselle min
Swaz hie gat umbe
Pity them, dancing, circling,
round they go, without a man
for summer show,
without a man
all summer long,
let it not be so.
10. *Were diu werlt alle min*
I'd throw away the world
to have the Queen of England
by my side, and hold her fast.

II. In Taberna
11. *Estuans interius*
Drifting, morose
nowhere to climb
nothing to do
but linger on and on
and wander around;
I join the lechers,
soak my dried-up self
in wine, a boat
without a rudder,
a leaf that's lost
in Time.

12. *Olim lacus colueram*
Once a beauty, graceful as a swan
now I'm roasted black as stew
for those with teeth enough to chew.
Curses be! They still have
teeth enough to chew.
13. *Ego sum abbas*
Here's to the abbot
well-drowned in wine
whose friends lose their garments
when out to dine.
14. *In taberna quando sumus*
In a tavern
in a stupor
gaming tables stained in wine
dwell the gamblers, pimps and harlots
and, of course, my concubine.

Some drink, some gamble,
many play, and others dandle.
Win a cloak -- lose a habit,
Death's remote -- forget about it.

Here's to the dice, may Bacchus win!
Here's to Christians who always sin!
Here's to the soldier who still has his pay!
Here's to our friends who have gone astray!
(Lucky fellows in every way.)

III. Cours d'Amours
15. **Amor volat undique**
Love is everywhere
so is loving,
some are matched

(alone's no fun)
some are snatched
(but I'm alone).
16. *Dies, nox et omnia*
Give an old man a kiss
to keep me young --
She gave me a miss --
I might as well hang.
17. *Stetit puella*
18. *Circa mea pectora*
In a red tunic stands that beauty
give me a chance and I'd know my duty;
give me a glance and she'd be my booty.
19. *Sie puer cum puellula*
20. *Veni, veni, venias*
21. *In trutina*
Girls and boys in hay do play
lingering, loving, in every way.

But come, roly-poly,
you're pretty and sweet
your hair is curly
your eyes are bright;
come, roly-poly, be my delight.
(I'll bear the burden of your submission
but won't admit it's your decision.)
22. *Tempus est iocundum*
23. *Dulcissime*
New love, new love
I'm on fire
every 'yes' will bring me joy
and every 'no' increase the pyre.
Let me die -- let me give,
let me give -- let me die.
Oooooh! Let me lie.

Blanziflor et Helena
24. *Ave formosissima*
Hail to you, so pure!
Hail to you, demure!
Light of the world!
Rose of my life!
Praise to your beauty
both day and night.

Fortuna Imperatrix Mundi
25. *O Fortuna*
O Fortune, O Fortune
like a moon, full and new
weep for us all
and despair of her rule.

The Rise of Bureaucracy:
The Westminster Paving Act (1761)

Whereas several squares, streets and lanes within the city and liberty of Westminster are ill-paved, uncleaned, and not duly lighted;

Whereas present methods prescribed by law are ineffectual;

Whereas it would tend greatly to the benefit and safety of the inhabitants if said squares and streets were purified of obstructions and annoyances;

May it therefore please your Majesty to appoint commissioners and order their meeting at Westminster Bridge on the first Thursday after the passing of the Act;

At which time fifteen commissioners, or more, may elect twenty others;

eleven present may fill vacancies by death, or refusal to act;

eleven may appoint clerks, treasurers, receivers, surveyors, and such officers as they deem necessary.

They may also appoint others.

Advice to Parents: London 1747

Shagreen-case makers fit cases for watches, tweezers, and chests for plate. There is some ingenuity in the business and reasonable profit to the Master. A youth requires neither strength nor previous education.

Trunk makers are noisy. They also make leather-buckets and return a reasonable profit. A lad must be a dunce who cannot acquire the skills in less than seven years. A moderate share of strength is needed.

A box-maker is a bungling joiner, with more strength than brains.

The needle-maker need not be as acute as the instruments he makes. his skill is his just temper of the steel.

Pin-making is but poor business and monies from pins but slight reward.

The cork-cutter requires but a sharp knife, and is worth no boy's while to learn.

The brush-maker: the age fit for binding is from twelve years up. Education will not influence its art.

Of rags for mops: Ragmen make a genteel living by it.

The silk-weaver's boy may be bound at eleven, but often younger, more to advantage the Master than anything they may learn of the trade.

The silk-thrower employs mostly women on but small wages. It is very profitable to the Master and requires but small ingenuity. Many women make good bread if they refrain from drinking and sotting away their time and senses.

Of the copper-smith. His work is laborious and apprentices need much strength, and ought to live by themselves being boisterous and noisy.

Wax-chandlers. A nasty greasy business. Profits alone atone for it. Physicky people find much difficulty breathing the scent, but it is healthy enough, and only a few die of consumption. Sealing-wax and wafers are deemed a more genteel trade.

The Almshouse

When Thomas Chapman died in 1602
he left a benefice for twelve good men of prayer
to be nourished until the Lord's Will
brought them to His Side.

So my uncle Ned (actor turned sailor),
who said he once knew Sir Beerbohm Tree,
applied for nourishment, aged seventy-three.

"Your Grace," he wrote, "prayer saved my life on the
Titanic,"
which intrigued the Bishop so, that early in spring,
        reviewing his winter losses,
he placed old Ned on the sunniest side of Chapman's Close
with a window to frame my uncle's pride;
a sloop in a bottle and Buddha from Ceylon.

The Bishop, not above believing, came visiting . . .
"Saved by prayer you say.
        I'd have thought a lifeboat more sure,
though, of course, your courage is the Lord's due."

"Quite right, your Grace, but it happened so.
I had just turned in,
     a bit unsteady after a heavy meal,
and was praying at an open porthole -- praying for land,
        or at least a nearby shore,
when suddenly the ship awoke, shook off her drowsy sleep -
and in a trice I was through that porthole,
soon joined by the chapel's altar
        also at sea.

Night on that altar-raft was cold,
but at early dawn that Buddha in my window floated by.
I reached through the fog to rescue Him,
and by chance, caught a line to an empty boat
    with stores and flares still dry,
      and as you see, survived.

If you should ever be in need, your Grace,
I'm sure He'd let me lend you Him."

the blinding day, and

WE   BUY   TIME . . . .

Bird-Cage

I have a friend
who had the misfortune
to be locked inside a poem
        recently

Something had arrested him
but he didn't stop there,
he had to go through with it,
statement, counter-statement and form.

He was charged,
    spent the whole night inside,
wondering how it sounded to speak up
clearly and say 'the truth, the whole truth,
and nothing but the truth.'

His friends still visit him
but they don't quite understand
why he's waiting to be caught again
inside another.

Do not write
  too clearly
lest you move
Earth and Heaven
  before their time.

Half my life spent
  attaching my heart
    to this and that,
The rest,
  detaching it again.

-Abû Talîb Kalîm (Persian)
(d. 1651/2?)

The monastery clock seems to chime
    slower
    and
        slower
        and
            slower
after midnight.
    Surely, it is behind the times.

A Question of Temperament

Do you play your dramas
Greek and Japanese:
Gods, masks, and antiphons,
giants and sprites, all
compelling passion's tragedies
then claiming ironic rights

or do your fingers
tiptoe and glide
playing gentle ragas,
then subside?

Dear Buddha:
be gentle to those with passions
and compassionate
on those without.

The Countess At The Bar

I

For many years after Emile's death
I didn't like onions,
rubbing off the parchment with my thumb
no paring-knife can circumscribe as well,
and the tears . . .
thirty-seven years
of tarte à l'oignon, without a smile,
except the final one beauticians contrive,
overreaching life,
and humoring what's left.

But Joel . . .
I still remember him, from Bermuda.
Friends tried to put me off:
". . . and at your age,
he's only a boy . . ."
Of course I knew jealousy
prompted their dismay.

All that concern for my well-being . . . .
afraid I might squander wealth on him
instead of the parties
I gave there at first . . . .
and those favors
wasted on that lot,
but it's tiring being nice.

II

He went to Maine I hear
into the snows of local politics
far from my grasping crowd
so proud of their avarice.
But who has ever checked
a country cord of wood
knows more about prehensile greed
than my gang did.
But it wasn't for him - but me -
and that's not a waste.
Of course,
he phantasized as most men do . . . .
I never could. That's why
the few wines I keep
are always good.

III

Why that mirror there?
It's so unkind, and even
with me slumping
behind the menu-holder,
my brow, now corduroy,
still shows, but what's a face
with nothing to entice it to.
Love so long disused can wrinkle too
besides there's nothing worth the enticing.
Some pains drive us to doings
that make them worse.
But how to renew this dried-up fig
not even a wasp could pollinate
where only pain outwits self-loathing.

IV

His final evening here Joel was sad
his mother was dying; he wanted her to go
yet felt ashamed. With her still alive
his liberty was at risk.
"It's all for the best, I suppose,"
but he wanted the release.

Never replace a mother too quickly . . .
Besides he always seemed to want
more than that - baby and man in one
With nothing to be passionate about.

I always place a man
where he can preen
in case I'm bored.
But they're all so vain
they never feel the need
the way we do . . . .
My left profile
suits me best, the cheekbone's higher
and earrings from my left lobe
always swing more freely
but Joel . . . . he wouldn't care.
Women know they will age
but men never believe they must.
No mirror now will bother him,
north face of the Eiger, I used to say.

Funny how I remember that . . . .
I once dreamt I was a mountaineer,
almost the first woman up its face,
but I returned to a jeering crowd
because I wouldn't drink to celebrate.

That's why I turned to wine,
the best bottlings at first, but now,
the vintage is only mine,
eighty-three, a good year,
but I miss my vine.
His touch was firm but soft,
like marble, almost pliant . . . .
Did Rodin get his medium wrong?

So I've turned to onions again,
mostly pickled - I hadn't thought of that;
but I miss my Bermuda,
so white and sweet.

V

One Sunday morning at mid-day Mass
while kneeling, her jaw dropped.
The funeral was bare, her gang so old
they didn't care . . .
Two managed to phone her lawyer (just in case),
'Did she have any close relatives
we might write to . . . ?' not daring to ask
what she had left and to whom.
Who knows? She might have left
her friends a little something,
a souvenir . . . of what?

The lawyer thanked them for their solicitude,
'The will was simple, dated a year ago:
"I leave everything,
wheresoever and whatsoever,
to Joel who will know as he always did,
how best to use whatever he has."'

The estate was large, mostly cash,
some trinkets (the Salvation Army sort).
The lawyer did well out of it,
but Joel got a final nibble at last,
at least his third wife did -
or so the barman said.

The Peterloo Massacre Witnessed:
Manchester (1819)
or Kent State

With respect to the sticks:
I saw a column pass by Mosley Street
and one (not two) in ten had sticks fresh-cut,
walking-sticks as country folk wear,
not carried as muskets,
not clubs and bludgeons, as some would say.
One would have expected more.

Then came the cavalry across St. Peter's Field,
    a woman drowned (child killed)
    a man upward of seventy (two arms broken)
as they turned him against our cottage wall.

Had the crowd given way
    not a sword would have swung
    nor any cuts been given.
The dust arose
    and I could not see all that passed.

161 sabre-wounds were counted
140 to young girls and women.
However, it gives me great pleasure
to state my belief
    that the yeomanry are incapable
        of acting with deliberate cruelty.

Tsunami

"Last night a major eruption
fifteen miles south of the Azores,
seventeen miles deep
was monitored in Madrid at 8.3
on the Richter scale.
Expect heavy Atlantic rollers
on the East Coast of the United States.
We will keep you informed."

A tsunami with plenty of space and time
to build and roll right over the eastern seaboard.
Hiroshige's fishing boat again!
How far inland will it go.
No more Long Island, New York'll catch it
Boston and Philly too.
I wonder what will happen to Washington
with all its low-lying politicians
on the run to Governmental hideouts,
leaving their families behind.

It may be seven years off,
                or a hundred thousand,
                even a few million.
Inevitable geologists say,
so why do anything?
Just lie back, think of sunny shores,
wave goodbye to office hours,
e-mail and the seventeen copies
you deliberately forgot to send out
                two days ago.

My theology is all cosmology now
with some geology,
                and very little else.

A Prayer For Salvador Dali

Dear painter of many Crucifixions
who lowers a head to lose a face,
obscuring palms with nails
large enough to hide the lines of Fate.

Grant us the joy of imperfection
and the suspension of all prediction.

The Gardner's Offering

When your spirit's taut
and the muscles of the mind
stretched out beyond recoil,
your body, scaffolding around a pit,
      then,
then will I bring you snowdrops,
crocus, daffodils and Spring,
untwist your every torque till slack
      and turn you
from staring at Heaven's back.

Mrs Chaney, or Consequences

I

She always sang boisterously at Sunday School,
corncake and macaw in unison
saluting the happy morn.
"I'm an example to my little Christian horde,
singing lustily so they too
        will raise their voices
        in sweet harmony
        to our Lord."

"Don't forget to blow your noses
before the service begins,
and Julia, don't sniggle at sermon-time
it upsets the minister
distracting us from all God's word;
and as for that smell of peppermint
last Sunday -- it's disrespectful."
"But, Mrs Chaney, God loves incense.
How does he know the difference?
Besides, it helps us sing."
"Don't ask silly questions.
Of course He knows. he knows everything...
He knows you always ask silly questions...
Here's the procession, don't forget
to bow as the Crucifix passes by."

One Easter Sunday the incense
compelled Mrs Chaney to cough a little,
        forget her mission
                and sneeze.
We too cleared our throats (in sympathy, of course),
grinned or giggled into flowery handkerchiefs

75

(no kleenex on Sundays);
while Julia handed round
more peppermints under our hymn-books
and devoutly bowed as the Cross went by.

After church on Sundays Mrs Chaney
restocked her bird-house,
divided clumps of her tallest daffs,
re-aligned tulips, mumbling to them
her encouragement:
    'Soldiers of Christ arise
    And put your armor on';
then spread manure
    lightly round the 'mums.

Julia always remembered
Mrs C.'s favorite elegy:
"Funerals become our garden's purpose
with a new Soul now in Heaven.
There is no sorrow in death,
mourning is mere selfish indulgence
    no Christian should enjoy."

II

Julia told me all this
while rehearsing Brahms' *Requiem*.
I'm a mediocre bass, Julia alto.
Six months later we were married
in the courthouse opposite the church.

Another generation,
but even with three children
Brahms is unlucky.
Tommy is learning the trumpet:

Vivaldi and Pop,
the others can't get a note;
and every Sunday as Julia passes the church
to take them swimming,
I stay home, relax with a beer
and snooze
         with Tommy gone.

On their return the kids run ahead
while she drops by Mrs C.'s place.
The daffs are smaller now,
unkempt clumps, the tulips gone.
"Hello Mrs Chaney," I can hear her call.
"I've brought you some peppermint patties."
"What's that, my dear, I'm a bit deaf now."
"Peppermint patties, for you."
"How kind, my favorites, I love their aroma,
I'll have one every evening
just to remind me... What was I saying?
I'm padding pot-holders for the church bazaar.
They don't fetch much but they keep my fingers
                    nimble
Just back from church?"
"No. I took the kids swimming,
but I still sing... alto, you remember...
Brahms' favorite voice."
"Ah, then surely you still are praising God
for that fine voice you always had."
"Oh no, Mrs Chaney, that's not why I sing,
      I have a great voice
      and I love singing."
"Well, my dear, praising Him without knowing...
that's the next best thing, I suppose...
D'you think green would go best with red
over the padding...?"

Omar S. Pound

From *Inside & Out*

Politician (retired)

Listen to those seagulls squawking,
some mew while others croak,
they think they're all in politics.
But with your visiting
        and all your talky-talk
they've missed their morning scraps.

I always give them something
to keep my ducklings safe;
though every spring
they swoop at the smallest,
        usually the last in line
on their first drunk tumbling
        to the sedge's edge
        and swallow it whole;
a gullet full of fluff...
and sometimes
        they eat a guillemot.

I fed a kittiwake last winter,
knowing what he'd gobble up
        next spring.

But then I eat their eggs,
        the usual quid pro quo
        (the first two sets, no more,
        the third I let them hatch).

One gull swoops,
    they all dive down
    and drown the waters
    with their scavenging
    and fishy politics;
    but they can't be bought,

        squawk, squawk,
        they are never bought.

Two Winnebago Moments

1

Lightning spun, thunder
rolled and bounced
across the ground
among us.

The Gods were angry
so I shot my son,
and as he died I took his name,
a keepsake for us all.

2

We often played dice
for the garments of the dead,
but that was before
the Christians came.
Now we dare not.

Our songs for gambling
and for love are so alike.

Moon-Catch in Snowlight

We were strangers who both knew
our crisp tread on new snow
an impediment to
      listening inside the night.

So we stopped to view the moon practising
different kinds of dawn behind the hill,
then it broke away:

      Oak catches it in her branches
      throws it to Birch. Birch lobs
      it slowly over Apple's head to
      Poplar, who passes it behind
      Byrd's Hill.

      and the snow turns blue again.

Baghdad: On a Bus To the Front

When the sword is broken
       the hilt is there,
when the hilt is gone
       the scabbard is there;
when the scabbard is done
       the belt is there;
when the belt is gone
       the Soul is there.
And when the Blacksmith
       calls my Soul,
       He mends the sword.

The archbishop appointed Erkenwald to be bishop in the city of London, whose life and conversation was taken for most holy. . . . For until this day his horse litter, wherein he was wont to be carried when sick and weak, doth daily cure such as have agues or are diseased, but also the chips and pieces that are cut off from it and brought to the sick folk, are wont to bring them speedy remedy.

Bede, Hist. Eccles. IV, 6

Saint Erkenwald

In London
    not long since Christ
        was crossed for Christendom
a bishop blessed the temple haunts
        of heathen whores.
His name was Erkenwald,
        and *Poules* his church,
re-faithed by him,
        they call St. Paul's.
He hurled out idols
        or named them newly, Saxon saints,
familiar to his flock.
He bundled out the randy retinue
        of Hengist's hordes,
and swore to build the Church anew
        to welcome back the Lord.

He hired rough-masons
        each crewed to haul and hew,
and master-masons
        with lads to twit and tease
and hone, and cheer the chisels on.
Then, marshalling men of brawn
        with belted bellies,
pick and pole probed ruin's mound

to found Christ's firmest foothold in the land.
And there, deep down,
      poles poked, picks stuck and snapped,
they'd struck a marble tomb.
       'Sarcophagus,'

        the clerics said,
garnished with gargoyles,
      with lumps where they lacked,
garnet eyes and agate tongues,
and round the tomb letters,
      some silver, some gilded with gold.
The Dean thought them Latin, others Greek,
two bundled the letters in lots
    till heads were in heat,
      and saw many a word that wasn't.
One read the writings of Thor.
    A few thought them odd,
      with no meaning at all.

Wives plucking pigeons
      and whispering awe,
elbowed forward
    for more of the marvel,
      which, wound round with wonder,
soon spread,
'Sir Kofagus has been found gelded,
      on a litter of gold.'

Lads leapt from learning
turners tossed tools aside
all vied for a viewing
from a dray nearby.

Then beadles and burghers

all breathless and bossy,
bellies an asset in parting the crowd,
cried out clearly,
"The Clerk of the Works is here.
Move over!

   Make way for his muster and mare!"
And pushed women aside
    with their parsley and wares,
proud to be first to peep inside.
"The lid must be lifted and laid just here...."

So crowbar and jemmy jostled the joints,
Some swore and sweated like clay,
    others advised and orated,
till silenced, dismayed:
  'A corpse is there, buried, and undecayed.'

Look how he lies! Face freckled, nostrils hairy,
flesh unfaulted, unfrumenting, unwormed,
and those cheeks!
    might have swallowed the sun!
Eyes lightly lidded, a falcon at rest,
brows brown and bushy,
    chin covered in down.

A girdle of gold gripped the groin,
acorns, falcons, yarrow and lilies
embroidered the cloak
  with devout short stitches closely sewn.
New silk on wool,
  hood edged with ermine whiter than shell,
linen well laundered,
    not a flea in the folds
     of the wormless weeds,

flesh unfaulted,
        as I mentioned before,
and deeds?
        Still unsorted out by the Lord.

"Send for the Bishop,
       town troubles
            truant trickery
               maybe a miracle,
any excuse, but bring him back quickly."

Three messengers, packed up and off, heard
Erkenwald was last seen,
        eastward-bound,
to care for morals (some said)
in an Essex nunnery, near Witham, I think.

Lightly loaded they soon caught him up,
what with his walnuts, cheese and new pestle,
but 'Erk,' as the kitchens called him,
        hurried them back:
"We've a vigil tonight,
       I'll follow tomorrow.
Take Broomwit the Beadle
    to tone down town tensions till I get back."

At dawn, the abbess, with blessings,
her own white horse,
herbs, honey and ale,
bustled him off to London.

Now Broomwit,
        worthy and waiting as ever,
had serviced their lips with awe.
          No use!

When the Bishop dismounted,
    all shouted, 'Good old Erk!'
with a catcall or two from the dray nearby,
as ostlers brought water, a blanket and hay.

A quick blessing...
    then prayers and some sleep.
But tired in marrow,
      visions vied with his vigil
as faith unfurled
   a view of the dead in a Heathen world,
where,
   deprived of all senses
no river-mists,
    no toll of the bell,
no garlic fritters,
    no faithful foregathered,
they must be in HELL.
'Dead,
   without decay,
      body uncorrupted....'
'If Christian,
   how come the delay?'
'O Magnum Mysterium....But wait!
      Is he dead?'
   For in death all knowing dies,
   and only what we cannot know
   proliferates.

Ere vigil and visions were lost, Matins rung,
all gathered for Mass in the autumn sun.

More blessings, (more meaning now),
Cheapside filled
   as the choir hallelujah'd

its way to St. Paul's.
"His two favorite rites," a burgher said,
"An Erkenwald blessing, and a Mass for the Dead."

"Beloved Beacons of the Lord," the Bishop began...
then stopped.
      "He loves your loud laughter,
          but, dearest friends, is a Soul lost?"

Mass over,
      he turned to the corpse to talk.
Lid lifted, he shortened his sleeve,
thumbed each eyelid up,
      till leadened by light they lowered.

"Dear Doers in Christ...
Nought's known but a heathen was buried here.
If Christian we'd know
      birthplace,
      marriage,
      and death,
but a Heathen...
      Who cares?
Uncaught by chronicle,
   all who might remember him
      have melted into Mystery.
O Magnum Mysterium et admirabile sacramentum."
His arms practiced preaching
      while his tongue took a rest.
"Out with it, Erk,"
      piped up Pete,
"Ask who he was.
      If he ain't dead, he oughta know that."
"Oh, Pete,"
      said the Bishop,

"don't tangle your tenses."
and coughed:
"Who were, er..., who are you?

The world's weight.
What corner did you bear?
How long, and why here?
Your wealth?
Whose was it?
Who has it now?
And, er..., your Faith?
How near to Hengist's hordes or Jesus' joy?"

"What light!" the corpse replied,
and with that,
Tom darted out to tell Cheapside and Molly,
"That damned body answered the Bishop back!
Erk's right after all! A miracle!
That means more faithful to our fair,
our takings up,
and tithings, too.
More graves to dig,
new thongs for sandals,
real relics this year, not fakes,
more mead
and
lots more Molly."

The baker and brewer (brothers) heard Tom.
"Alert the lads!
More saffron in the buns,
more salt and seasonings to feed their thirst.
Off that dray, you louts.
We'll need it now
for those we parch in service of their Lord.

Pilgrims must pay for piety.
That Bishop's still braying,
   'O Magnum Mysterium,'
      a miracle perhaps to fools,
      but deeds like these come easy to the Lord."

The Bishop beamed,
   "Indeed, all things come easy to the Lord,
   when the Prince of Paradise unlocks His Might."

The corpse sighed...
"Don't fret,"
      said the Bishop,
"We'll soon have you out,
        but I'm not sure how."

Said body, "If I knew the world's weight
     I'd tell what I bore,
but none knows another's burden,
     save the ass.
How long here?
     Any man's number might guess it right,
800 years perhaps,
     but I knew from the grave Christ's birth,
the earth warmed up
     and violets grew.

"Who am I?
     Who knows?
        No one cares!
Your records won't show,
     I used them enough to know that.
My wealth?
     No joyless needs
       I wanted less than I had.

Possessions possessed me now and then,
   with half my life spent
      attaching my heart
        to this and that,
           the rest, detaching it again."

April the Thirtieth, in 693,
Erkenwald died, of chest fever,
      as many do,
        attending each other's funerals.
March thinned him so, and even Spring
failed to luster the bones or brighten skin...
but the earth warmed up
        and violets grew.

They buried him Monday,
        market-day it was,
Each limb wrapped in linen,
        his own Coptic comb,
new sandals from Pete,
        a wool alb from Witham,
a girdle of gold from the Cheape;
on his heart
        his own amber drop,
full of fleas and a fern
        in the form of a Cross;
on his head,
        an osier crown made by Molly.

And over it all a cloak
   embroidered with falcons and flowers,
      yarrow and lilies in tiny stitches.
None knew whence it came,
'A gift from a friend for a favor in life.'
        Who knows?

Broomwit, still waiting and worthy,
　　puttered and hovered,
scraping grease-marks and smudges,
as coffin was covered
　　　　and well-lidded down.
Molly whispered to Tom,
"Will that hold him under?
　　Don't want him up and around.
Might come when it's in,
　　　　and he might lose my crown.
And that heathen the Bishop corrupted
　　　　and turned to dust?
Will he do the same for us?"

Tom's answer was lost as all crowded round
for relics...
　　　　a sliver of cedar
　　　　　some lint from his gown.
All envied his ivory comb, twin-edged,
　　　　teeth tapered and worn,
but if I know Broomwit,
　　　　it's still in the tomb.

Broomwit as ever brushed longings aside!
　　"Dear Sisters and Brothers.
　　　　Why relics?
　　　　　You store in each eye,
　　　　　　Dear Lovers in Christ,
　　　　　　　a tear to baptize.
A relic of Christ in each cleric of God.
　　　　You are your own reliquary.
　　　　All praise to the Virgin Mary. Amen."

Erk always said,

'Broomwit's best when caressing a crowd.'
The thunder amen'd with the monks,
                again and again,
hail flailed the ground,
and freed from a need for relics now,
all solemnly smiled,
                wandered off
                        and withdrew.
One of the deacons put two hairs back,
                like Molly's, but who knew that.

To tether this tale:
bells boomed as many and then as one
as Saint Erkenwald joined The Unpaganed One,
name still a mystery,
                save to a few,
        and to
                The Fourth Bishop of London.

Broomwit, even with Spring come alive,
suddenly tired and died.
They buried him
                in a tomb, waiting and worthy,
with letters incised in silver and gold:

SERVUS DEI

which is, 'Servant of God,' I'm told.

Omar S. Pound

A Coin Given To A Friend

I gave away my childhood once,
a coin, smooth as a mushroom after rain,
found where the beach
        was slippery green
and iodine popped between my toes;
the silver's silk sea turbulence had calmed
and only the shadow of a distant queen,
still hugging matter, revealed
        her revenue and rectitude.

Yes. I gave away my childhood once,
dated 1587 to another child
whose only private hour
        was stringing out the sunset
                into night.

Mr. Joyce On Trial

Prosecuting lawyer:
　　Can I see your driving-license, Mr. Joyce?
Mr. Joyce: No
Prosecuting lawyer: Your Honor,
　　May I treat this witness as a hostile witness?
Judge: Yes, you may.
Prosecuting lawyer:
　　Can I see your driving-license?
Mr. Joyce: I don't know, not unless you have ESP.
Prosecuting lawyer: What is ESP?
JJ: Extra Sensory Perception.
Prosecuting lawyer:
　　What does that have to do with your driving-
license?
JJ: I don't know whether you can see it or not, unless you
can see through aether and walls. It's not in this room.
Prosecuting lawyer:
　　Very well. I would *like* to see your driving-license.
JJ: You may. It's at home.
Prosecuting lawyer:
　　Very well, with the Court's permission I would like
Mr. Joyce to go home to fetch it.
JJ pulls out an airline time-table.
JJ: I'll leave tomorrow evening for Trieste from LaGuardia,
and be back in a few days. I'll have to look for it.
Judge: Are you sure it's there?
JJ: Yes, Your Grace. -- Sorry, that was a graceless mistake.
I didn't mean to treat you so dishonorably.
Judge: And when you come back I won't have you and Mr.
Slipkin quibbling over words. you must stop this quibbling.
Oh! [*pause*]
Lunch recess. Court is adjourned.
You gentlemen will report to my chambers after lunch.

Confinement, or
A Modern Philoctetes

Don't leave me here
where even the soothing silk
of anorexic bars of light
corrode my face, rust my skin,
clutter up my pores
with more sorrow than any man
            ordered to live alone
            should bear.

I was not born to burst
            and spill resentment anywhere,
but here
            I have no birthdays, Holy Days,
or even Fasts for feasting on my Soul
or whatever is left of me
            to contaminate.

I did what I did.
It was declared a crime,
            but only
            if you deny the Soul,
(uncatalogued in law and hard to find,
somewhere... anywhere...
            in the shelf of life.)

Even in uniform, I could not kill,
            would not,
            and refused again.
Details don't matter...
They say I let my buddies down.

Many died,
while those in public places
made martial speeches
to curb my stand.

Dangling my
              "Bomb Bosnia Now" button,
'Scarface,' our prison cat,
              pats it, traps it,
              pounces, hides from it,
and to tease me,
pretending it's not there
with nonchalant feline disdain,
while I, too, pretend
              it's all a game.

My neighbor and too many friends
enjoyed toasting my love-poems
in the wine I had bought
to share with you.

My One and Only Love

And there he was
up the ladder with a bucket of whitewash
in one hand, and hanging on to his trousers
                    with the other.
Don't worry about the trousers, I shouted,
don't waste the paint - and whoops!
                    all over me,
          and his trousers down.

We got engaged two weeks later,
          and look where I am now,
four of them, all boys - all terrors.
But he won't do any more painting around the house
says, at his age, it's undignified.

One-Word Poems

Horses of the Apocalypse

Nightmares.

Subjunctive Power

Might.

The Playwright

Brevis esse laboro obscurus fio
                              -Horace

I try to be brief,
turn novel into play,
            to poem,
thence to epigram or phrase;

reflect and rest awhile,
to hear the phrase uncoil,
spring to epigram or verse
and lastly
            flow to play again.

The Dying Expatriot

Let me hear English again,
its roundabouts, wheezings,
and niggling nonsense
    sometimes keen.

Tell me of silver birch in dusk's long alert,
pink chestnut, foxgloves and yarrow,
bells and starlings across an English lawn,
and sparrows stealing from the thatch.

Let me hear the language to pity men in,
here, where sun and rain
divide their time more fruitfully
and death is merely a transient thing.

Said Wasp To Bee

Said wasp to bee:
they loathe me
stone my nest
smoke me out
and even pay
for cyanide
to move me;

but you,
with your hexagons
and pollen dances
they house in luxury.

Said bee: to sting
and still be loved
you must give honey.

Nosrat kasemi Mazanderani (Persian)
b. 1911

Omar Shakespear Pound

Son of poet Ezra Pound and vorticist painter Dorothy Shakespear, Omar Pound was born in Paris, France, in 1926. He was reared by his grandmother, novelist Olivia Shakespear, in England, where he attended school until age sixteen. He left in 1943 to train in hotel management, working in a large London hotel. In 1944 he was bombed out when the house in which he was living fell on him. In 1945 he joined the U.S. Army and served as a GI in France and Germany until 1946.

He attended his father's school, Hamilton College, in Upstate New York, where he studied anthropology and French. After college he studied Islamic History and Persian at the School of Oriental and African Studies in London. He returned to the United States and received a Rockefeller Grant to study at the Institute of Islamic Studies at McGill University in Montreal, Canada, where he studied classical Arabic and continued his graduate work in Islamic History under Professor Wilfred Cantwell Smith, the distinguished scholar of Islamics. After receiving his graduate degree, he went into teaching in Boston (1957-1962) and was invited to become headmaster of the American School in Tangier, Morocco. After three years he returned to England to lecture in a technical college in Cambridge for about thirteen years before returning to the US to teach English at Princeton University until he retired.

He was awarded an honorary doctorate in Humane Literatures from Lawrence University in Wisconsin.

In addition to his several volumes of poetry and translations, he has edited three volumes of his father's letters, the most recent with Oxford University Press. He is currently working on a collection of letters written in India in the 19th century. Over the years he has given numerous readings in the United States, Canada, England and Iraq.

Omar Pound and his wife Elizabeth live in Princeton, NJ, where he continues to write while battling cancer.